FLEXIBLE COMPENSATION
A Forward Look

Christine Seltz
Dale L. Gifford

AMA Management Briefing

AMA MEMBERSHIP PUBLICATIONS DIVISION
AMERICAN MANAGEMENT ASSOCIATIONS

Library of Congress Cataloging in Publication Data

Seltz, Christine, 1950-
Flexible compensation.

(AMA management briefing)
1. Non-wage payments—United States. 2. Compensation management—United States. I. Gifford, Dale L., 1950- . II. Title. III. Series.
HD4928.N62U68 1982 658.3'22 82-18414
ISBN 0-8144-2272-1

This Management Briefing has been distributed to all members enrolled in the Insurance and Employee Benefits Division of the American Management Associations. Copies may be purchased at the following single-copy rates: AMA members, $7.50. Nonmembers, $10.00. Students, $3.75 (upon presentation of a college/university identification card at an AMA bookstore). Faculty members may purchase 25 or more copies for classroom use at the student discount rate (order on college letterhead).

First Printing

About the Authors

Christine Seltz is a consultant with Hewitt Associates at the firm's general offices in Lincolnshire, Ill. She has written extensively for the firm on various subjects in the employee benefit and compensation field. Ms. Seltz holds a B.A. from Skidmore College.

Dale L. Gifford is an actuary with Hewitt Associates and practice manager for the firm's services in flexible compensation. Also located in the Lincolnshire office, he serves as a resource to the entire organization on the consulting and technical aspects of flexible compensation program design and implementation. Mr. Gifford holds a B.A. in business administration from the University of Wisconsin and is a Fellow of the Society of Actuaries.

Acknowledgments

The authors wish to acknowledge the substantial contribution of numerous members of their firm to the development of this management briefing. The material represents a compendium of the flexible compensation consulting activities undertaken by Hewitt Associates over the past decade.

Contents

1

Why the Interest in Flexible Compensation?

The past decade has seen considerable interest in the concept of flexibility in compensation and benefits. Throughout much of the 1970s, both TRW and Educational Testing Service had flexible programs in operation, and an impressive amount of publicity surrounded American Can's adoption of a program in 1978. Discussion of flexible compensation also surfaced among social critics and business thinkers. Alvin Toffler, in *The Third Wave,* concluded that there is no one set of incentives and benefits that motivates the full spectrum of the workforce.

Peter Drucker, in *Managing in Turbulent Times,* urged employers to recognize the heterogeneity of the workforce by permitting employees to choose the benefits that best suit individual needs and circumstances. In recent lectures, Drucker has advocated choice-making in benefits and compensation as a means by which employers also might start the process of getting out from under excessive overhead costs.

Until recently, however, there has been more talk than action. The reasons have been pragmatic. Tax legislation served as a major impediment; concern focused on whether employees would make wise decisions; employers were reluctant to take on a system thought to be inherently complicated.

The level of current activity suggests that much has changed. To date, over 30 companies in widely diverse industries have implemented programs, and over 100 more are in various stages of investigating the concept. Much of the activity would not now be occurring had legislation remained restrictive. But with the loosening of tax policy has come renewed interest in flexible compensation as a means of accomplishing certain goals in the human resource field.

APPEAL TO DIVERSE NEEDS OF THE WORKFORCE

The pattern of employee benefits in place today dates from the 1950s and the 1960s, when the "average" employee was a male with a nonemployed wife and dependent children. Benefits were provided on a "common denominator" basis—responding to the needs of the average employee by providing the same level of protection for all employees.

Unlike that pattern, the flexible approach to benefit planning allows a program to fit circumstances that differ among employees and that change over time as a result of events in a person's life—marriage, children, death of a spouse, and so on. Flexibility also makes compensation more useful by letting the individual allocate value to coverages truly needed or wanted.

Strong motivation for recognizing the differing needs of individuals and their changing needs over time comes from shifts in the demographics of the workforce. According to editors of *American Demographics* (July/August 1982), 1980 census data reveal some significant trends:

- *Increase in labor force participation by women.* Fully 50 percent of women over age 16 are in the labor force, up from 41 percent at the time of the 1970 census. Perhaps more significant is the influx of women with children. Of all mothers with children under age 6, 46 percent are now working—up from 31 percent in 1970. Of mothers with older children (ages 6 to 17), fully 63 percent are in the workforce.
- *Rise in the number of two-paycheck families.* Today, 54 percent of the nation's 59 million families have two or more workers. This

suggests that existing benefit structures are operating as intended in only the minority of family situations. Since 1970, the number of one-worker families has dropped from 40 percent to 33 percent.

- *Growth in the number of younger workers.* The age composition of the workforce is changing rapidly. Today, over half of the working-age population is under age 35. The values and priorities of this group probably differ considerably from those of groups ahead of them in the workforce.
- *Rise in educational levels.* The nation now has more highly educated residents than ever before. Fully 60 percent of people over age 25 now have at least a high school diploma, up from 52 percent in 1970. In addition, 32 percent of residents have attended college, including 16 percent who hold a degree. In contrast, only 21 percent of Americans had any college experience at the time of the 1970 census.

Changes in the age mix of the population, in the proportion of women employed outside the home, in the percentage of people with degrees, and in the composition of the typical family all point to the problem of how to please everyone with one set of compensation and benefit practices. Clearly, an employer could meet the needs and preferences of each segment of the workforce by continuing to expand the forms of pay and benefits provided. However, the 1980s appear to be stacking up as a different era for employee benefits—one in which control of cost is a legitimate employer objective. Flexibility provides a workable method for creating the desired diversity in benefits without expanding the employer's cost commitment.

CONTROL RISING BENEFIT COSTS

The employee benefit studies conducted by the U.S. Chamber of Commerce provide an historical perspective on the rise in employer cost for benefits. Among the constant sample of companies reporting regularly from 1959 to 1980, benefit expenditures have risen steadily: from 24.7 percent of payroll in 1959 to 41.4 percent in 1980. In dollar terms, benefit costs averaged $1,282 per employee in 1959; by 1980 the figure had soared to $7,633.

Another measure of upward momentum is the rise in *value* of benefits. When we factor out increases in benefit values attributable to rising compensation levels, we see that changes in plan design have enhanced the worth of benefits in real dollar terms. In the period from 1973 to 1981, based on Hewitt Associates Benefit Index™, values have risen 20 percent for all private employee benefits. Growth in the medical care area alone has fueled much of the overall increase. Net of the impact of inflation on the cost of providing medical benefits, the value of health care has risen over 30 percent during the period, due primarily to addition of coverages such as dental, hearing, and vision care. The dollar climb in benefit costs also has been accompanied by a shift in employee attitudes. Benefits have grown in meaning to the average worker, who now sees them as "entitlements" rather than as "gratuities." Benefits represent a "right"—to be protected against the financial hazards of working life. But within employee attitudes toward benefits lie the seeds of some of today's problems. From the typical employee's viewpoint:

- "Benefits should never be reduced. They are *mine,* with no take-aways tolerated."
- "The best benefit plan is one that replaces my loss completely, and at *no cost* to me. This is the standard against which I measure benefit provision."
- "Benefit programs at all companies keep increasing regularly. What have you (the employer) done for me lately?"

Herein lies the essence of conflict for the 1980s. *Are* benefits entitlements that come with the job? Or are they personnel costs subject to controls and changes as required for the economic good of the enterprise?

From the employer's viewpoint, benefits are a form of labor cost. Benefit levels should be kept high enough to remain competitive, but within cost bounds. They should adversely impact neither consumer prices nor shareholder return. When times are good, decent benefits should be maintained. When times are bad, benefit expansion needs to be curtailed. To an employer, bad times mean inability to afford more labor cost—especially the inflexible, overhead nature of most benefit costs.

When these two forces collide—employee desire for more and fuller benefit protection and employer need for cost containment—neither force is likely to triumph completely over the other. Rising employee expectations cannot be sustained in a faltering economy. Some employers who have tried to cut back benefits have met with employee or union resistance. Others have attempted to shift a greater proportion of the total cost to the employee—with the same result. Still others are opting for freezes in benefit levels. These efforts have had mixed success, since such a large proportion of benefit cost is subject to automatic escalation.

To many employers, flexible compensation presents a workable system for effecting compromise. The employee is given some say over how employer dollars are spent on his or her behalf. The employer gains some measure of control over the upward spiral in non-cash compensation costs. Increasingly, flexible compensation is being seen as a system for cost control that eliminates or minimizes the risk of alienating employees.

DELIVER COMPENSATION TAX-EFFECTIVELY

One effect of a well-designed benefit program is tax-effectiveness. Over the years, Congress has chosen to give tax-favored status to certain forms of compensation. Since employer dollars spent on certain items are tax-deductible to the employer and nontaxable income to the employee, paying someone in nontaxable form carries extra value. How significant is the issue of tax-effectiveness? Consider the situation of a typical employee during the 1970s.

According to AMA surveys, the average cost accountant in 1973 was earning $14,400 and paying taxes in the 27 percent marginal bracket. As pay rose over the years, so did the federal income tax bite. By 1980, average pay for the job was $24,600 and the marginal tax bracket had climbed to 34 percent. In 1981, average pay for the job was at $27,000, landing the person in a marginal tax bracket of 39 percent.

Changes that occurred during the 1973–1981 period included rapid growth in dental plans, increases in the number of savings plans and the level of company matching, introduction of vision and hearing care plans, Tax Reduction Act ESOPs (TRASOPs), and, of course, improvements in existing plans. Although changes were made partly in recognition of employee security needs, a major contributing factor was also that benefits represent a tax-effective form of compensation.

The flurry of interest currently in IRAs and Section 401(k) plans highlights the appeal of delivering compensation tax-effectively. These plans allow employees to set aside funds for later use in retirement and reduce current income tax liability in the process. The driving force behind the plans is deferral of taxes. Saving for retirement is the end result.

The rationale for the special tax advantages is that certain forms of pay and benefits have been judged by Congress to further social goals. For example, providing retirement benefits is considered a worthwhile social objective because it lowers the risk of the elderly becoming dependent on society in their postretirement years. Similarly, providing adequate health care coverage presumably prevents destitution caused by large and unexpected medical bills. For our nation's lawmakers, these are important principles—worthy enough to sustain revenue loss to the Treasury.

There have been some recent additions to the list of nontaxable benefits. Employer tax credits for payroll-based employee stock ownership plans (PAYSOPs) are justified on the basis of extending stock ownership to broad groups of employees. The various forms of saving for retirement—IRAs, 401(k) plans, H.R. 10 plans—are justified on the basis that deferring taxes on these items will help create investment capital and lead to increases in productivity, as well as provide reserves for individuals to use after retirement.

Group legal benefits and dependent care also fall into the category of nontaxable benefits if the employer pays the cost. There is also talk about adding further to this list. Adoption benefits and educational costs are two items receiving serious consideration. The underlying principle is again the same. The tax system is being used with increasing frequency to try to accomplish certain social ends.

Is the importance of tax-effectiveness likely to change in the future? Probably not. Consider the example of the cost accountant earning $27,000 in 1981. Although the 1981 tax act lowered rates for the next couple of years, a pay raise in 1982 nonetheless will boost the accountant into the 40 percent marginal tax bracket. Reductions will take effect starting in 1983, and the accountant's marginal tax rate will fall from 40 percent in 1982 to 36 percent in 1983 and 34 percent in 1984, after which time rates should begin to stabilize through indexing. Although the drop is a large improvement, it represents nothing more than a return to 1980 tax levels. That suggests that tax-effectiveness will remain an important issue.

Congress, alone, has the authority to decide what purposes are sufficiently noble to warrant favorable tax treatment. As the tax system is enlarged to meet social objectives, will the types of employer-pay-all plans similarly enlarge? This is a nice way to secure maximum tax-effectiveness—provided the employer has the money to pay the full cost of whatever forms of pay and benefits can be offered to employees. However, the economic realities of the 1980s indicate otherwise. Of the two ways to make a benefit program tax-effective—having the employer pay the full cost for all nontaxable benefits or having employees elect among taxable and nontaxable choices—momentum seems to be with the flexible, choice-making approach.

2

Flexible Compensation Defined

Flexible compensation is a system under which each individual has some choice as to the form of all or a portion of total compensation. Currently, there are no instances in which the individual is being given a choice as to *all* compensation. Employer objectives would not likely be achieved unless some portion of compensation were definitely allocated to cash income and another portion to some layer of employee benefit protection. Flexibility, then, is the creation of a *portion* of compensation that the individual can elect to have in cash or benefits or distribute among different types of benefits.

The basic concept of flexibility is not entirely new; some degree of choice-making has long existed in benefit plans. For example, many employers provide, in addition to a basic program applicable to all employees, optional coverages among which the employee can choose so long as he or she is willing to pay the cost of those optional benefits. The employer is providing both the advantages of group purchasing power and the availability of protection on a group basis regardless of health. However, the employee is paying the full cost. Optional life insurance or long-term disability coverages sometimes fall into this category of flexibility, as may dependents' life insurance and accidental death and dismemberment benefits.

A second form of existing flexibility is an arrangement under which supplements are available in addition to the standard program and the cost of the supplement is shared by employer and employee. For example, the company may provide basic medical care and offer major medical coverage with the employee and the company sharing the cost. A savings plan may permit an employee to save from 1 to 6 percent of salary with the company contributing $.50 (or more) for each dollar the employee deposits. In this type of flexible program, additional compensation is offered to the individual who chooses the supplementary coverage, but that additional compensation is not available to the individual who does not so choose.

A third type of flexibility, which serves as a model for the new types of programs currently being offered, involves an arrangement which provides the employee with a choice as to the form in which he or she will receive supplemental compensation. For example, in some profit sharing plans the employee has a choice whether to defer the entire allocation or to defer only a portion and receive the balance in cash. Some organizations provide employees a choice between taking a fourth week of vacation and receiving cash in lieu of the extra time off. The distinguishing characteristic of this type of flexibility is that the employee will receive equivalent value in one form or another.

Basic levels of compensation and benefits are applicable to all employees. A supplemental allowance in one form or another is made available and the employee is permitted to choose how to allocate that supplement.

The benefit reimbursement account and the benefit program/cash trade-off are two simple applications of this idea. The benefit reimbursement account is a credit reserve under which the individual can allocate flexible credits to pay for certain medical, dental, legal, and dependent care or other expenses not covered under the group program. Since employer payments for these expenses are deductible by the organization and not taxable to the individual, this process delivers tax-effectiveness on a noninsured basis. The benefit program/cash trade-off, on the other hand, simply allows individuals to elect full coverage under the standard benefit package or receive a cash payment equal to the cost of that program. Of course, any cash choice becomes taxable income.

Another approach, which can be implemented in a variety of ways, involves reshaping the employee benefit package. In concept, the funds for employees to spend as they wish are generated by shrinking existing coverage levels back to a "core" of benefits that applies uniformly to all employees. The core is set at levels needed to fulfill organizational objectives. For example, a company may find it unacceptable for an employee to retire without pension benefits or for the employee's family to be left without life insurance benefits in the event that he or she dies. The core benefits represent those levels of coverage necessary for the company to feel that adequate minimum protection is being applied in each area. The difference between the values of the old program and the new core are calculated and made available to employees in the form of a flexible benefit allowance. The individual may spend that allowance among various optional benefits provided under the program.

At first glance, the distinguishing characteristic of these various approaches to flexible compensation appears to be the latitude afforded employees to tailor pay and benefit packages to suit individual needs. Indeed, increasing the appeal and usefulness of benefits is a primary objective.

However, the more important distinction for the future is that flexibility enables an employer to set in place a system for managing total compensation costs. Flexible compensation provides the employer with a method for separating decisions on *form* of compensation from *cost*. One decision involves the forms of pay and benefits that will be provided, with employees choosing among those forms. The other decision involves the amount of money to be spent on pay and benefits, and that decision is reserved to the employer.

Consider how the concept of flexibility differs from the conventional approach.

With a conventional system, each discrete form of pay and benefits is directly supported by employer or employee funds, or some combination of the two. If the cost for a form of pay or benefit rises, there must be an increase in what is paid by the employer, the employee, or both.

Under a flexible approach, each optional form of pay or benefits has a specific price tag to be paid by those selecting that form. The price is related to actual experience and may be changed as necessary to pay the full cost. The employer's cost commitment is expressed in terms of

Exhibit 1. Flexible compensation. A system for paying people that separates decisions on forms of compensation from levels of employer cost.

Forms of Pay		*Employer Cost*
Year One		
• Medical	$____	____
• Death	$____	
• Time off	$____	
• Capital	$____	$2,000
accumulation	$____	____
• Cash	$____	
Year Two		
• Medical	$____	____
• Death	$____	
• Time off	$____	
• Capital	$____	$2,000
accumulation	$____	____
• Cash	$____	
• *Dental*	$____	
Year Three		
• Medical	$____	____
• Death	$____	
• Time off	$____	
• Capital	$____	$2,200
accumulation	$____	____
• Cash	$____	
• Dental	$____	
• *Dependent care*	$____	

total support for each employee in the pay and benefits system. Under this approach, an increase in the cost of a particular form of pay or benefits increases the price which employees must pay for that coverage, but does not necessarily increase the employer's cost commitment. In concept, the employer is driving a line of separation between the costs and prices for various components of pay, and the extent of employer commitment to support the program.

Assume an employer has $2,000 available to spend per employee per year on benefit production (Exhibit 1). Assume also that the $2,000 can be allocated by the employee in different amounts to purchase various levels of coverage within each benefit area. For example, life insurance is available in multiples of pay at age-related rates. Similarly, options are available within the medical area. For $300, the employee can purchase a medical plan with a large deductible and 80 percent co-insurance subject to a maximum out-of-pocket payment. For $400, the employee can have a plan with a smaller deductible and 80 percent co-insurance with a smaller out-of-pocket limit, while $600 will purchase first dollar coverage with 80 percent co-insurance on only some charges. (Prices for family coverage would be higher, depending on the number of dependents.) If the employee uses all the company money and wants additional coverages, then he or she pays for the coverage through payroll deduction. Conversely, an employee who elects not to use all the company money can flow excess amounts into a capital accumulation plan, or take the difference in cash. Any cash election, however, constitutes taxable income.

In Year One of the program's operation, the employee goes through a trade-off exercise to determine how best to allocate the company funds available. In Year Two of the flexible program's operation, a couple of events occur. First, experience indicates that the cost of the medical plan options must rise. Second, the company decides that an additional benefit option—dental coverage—would make the flexible program more attractive.

Similar events occur in Year Three. The cost of certain coverages rises and a new option is added—in this case, dependent-care assistance. Also in Year Three, however, the company decides to enrich the pool of flexible dollars in the program and adds $200 to each employee's flexible account. (In an actual case, the dollars probably would be expressed as a percentage of pay.) Employees have both another new option and more dollars to spend within the program.

What does the example illustrate? Throughout the years of the flexible program's operation, the employer's commitment to support the program remained independent of the prices charged employees. New options could be added, but not necessarily at the expense of the employer adding new dollars to the program. The employer added money when conditions warranted. In the meantime, employees rearranged existing employer dollars (or put in their own money) to pay for the coverages most desired. The employer separated decisions on the *form* of delivering benefits from the *cost* of providing coverage. In other words, the cost issue remained totally independent of the prices charged employees.

In reality, expectations of reducing or freezing employer expenditures at the time of introduction of a flexible system probably cannot be fulfilled. The reason is that individuals are being asked to change perceptions from "What have you—the employer—done for me lately?" to "How can I best use the money available to me now?" Getting across the concept of *trade-off* rather than add-on cannot be accomplished if an immediate employer objective is lower cost. If the individual does not perceive that the overall value of a new program is at least as great as the old program, there may be a feeling that the system is a shell game. Moreover, some degree of automatic escalation will continue to occur, forcing enhancement to the percentage of pay in the flexible program. But the advantage of a flexible system is that it takes a conscious management decision to raise the level of employer cost commitment. Over time, a flexible system will enable a company to slow down the rate of increase in employer expenditures for benefits.

3

Legal Framework

Recent changes in tax law have heightened employer interest in flexible compensation. A major new theme in tax policy represents a significant liberalization in government attitudes toward flexible compensation.

The major change involves a loosening of the doctrine of constructive receipt as it applies when employees can choose how employer money is to be spent on their behalf. Long a mainstay of tax policy, this doctrine says that if there is choice between taxable and nontaxable forms of compensation, or between value received now or later, income will be construed to be constructively received and tax now due. However, with respect to choices within benefit programs, the new doctrine says that tax is due currently only if the individual selects a taxable item, provided that the pattern of use of nontaxable forms in a group is not primarily for the benefit of highly paid participants. This is a remarkable change in policy—from a flat taboo to conditional permission provided the results of making choices are not discriminatory in practice. In essence, the "price tag" for favorable tax treatment of choice-making in benefits is a set of rules to prevent discrimination in favor of the highly paid.

Judged against the backdrop of prior legislative treatment of plans involving employee choice over employer monies, the nondiscrimination standard may be a small price to pay.

Until the early 1970s, the IRS had established no firm policy with regard to plans involving employee choice, except for a 1956 revenue ruling that essentially prohibited discriminatory operation. Individual salary reduction arrangements were in use, although primarily in the public sector. Cash option profit sharing plans, whereby an employee could elect an immediate cash payout in lieu of deferral of all or a portion of the employer contribution into a trust, were allowed. Even "cafeteria" plans, which permitted choices among taxable and nontaxable benefits or cash, were tolerated in a couple of instances. Regulations that would have eliminated these kinds of plans were proposed in 1972 but were never finalized.

Plans permitting employee choice essentially hung in limbo until 1974 when ERISA became law. Concerned about the threat to constructive receipt, Congress banned all kinds of plans permitting choice. Section 2006 of ERISA forbade the development of individual salary reduction plans, cash option profit sharing, and cafeteria plans containing taxable options until Congress could develop new rules for them. Existing plans could continue under previous provisions, but no new plans were permitted.

The employee choice issue surfaced again with the Revenue Act of 1978. Changes were made in the Internal Revenue Code less because of further congressional study, and more because of the need for permanent rules for the treatment of cafeteria plans providing taxable as well as nontaxable choices. Moreover, the cafeteria area was viewed as one where nondiscrimination rules could be advanced.

The 1978 Revenue Act permitted choices between taxable and nontaxable forms of compensation without constructive receipt of amounts that could have been received as taxable income but were instead spent for nontaxable benefits. Two types of trade-offs were permitted:

- Under Section 125, a cafeteria plan could provide choices between nontaxable benefits, taxable benefits, and cash. However, the plan would have to be nondiscriminatory with respect either to employer contributions to or benefits paid from the plan.
- Under Section 401(k), a cash or deferred profit sharing plan could provide an election between cash and deferral into a qualified profit sharing trust, but the pattern of deferral could not discriminate in favor of the highly paid.

Together, these two sections created the new legal framework for flexible compensation programs. But there were flaws. A Section 125 cafeteria plan could not contain a deferred compensation element. A Section 401(k) cash/deferred compensation arrangement could not include health benefits. These "oversights" were subsequently corrected by the flexible compensation legislation enacted in late December 1980.

The Miscellaneous Revenue Act of 1980 amended Section 125 to permit a cafeteria plan to include deferred compensation as an option, as long as the nondiscrimination requirements of Section 401(k) were satisfied. The 1978 and 1980 legislation now serve as the legal framework under which a flexible program may provide choices of welfare benefits, deferred savings, or cash in one program—all without application of constructive receipt.

Although legislation governing flexible compensation is in place, interpretive regulations and rulings are not. To date, only proposed regulations on Section 401(k) have been issued, with finalization not expected until late 1982. Some time in 1983 regulations on Section 125 are expected.

To some extent, the absence of implementation rules is hampering the spread of flexible compensation arrangements. Yet, many employers already have moved on line with programs. In large measure, the reasoning has been that each new promulgation from Washington seems less a new direction than a restoration or clarification of what had been allowed previously. The proposed regulations on Section 401(k) did contain surprises—such as allowing for savings through individual salary reduction. Yet, the legislation itself represents essentially restoration of the cash or deferred election that had been available in the period before ERISA. Similarly, regulations on Section 125 are likely to contain some new elements—such as making salary reduction available for group legal and dependent care benefits. But here again, Section 125 legislation is primarily a clarification of what had been allowed in selected cases.

Conceptually, the legislative framework makes no change in the employer's ability to take a tax deduction for benefit plans. Rather, the whole focus of the recent changes is to give the individual the ability to make decisions about how employer monies are to be spent on his or her behalf. The employer is no longer required to make decisions on behalf of employees in the aggregate.

The end result is more freedom for the employee to determine the form of compensation. Taxation will be based on what the employee selects. Constructive receipt will not be an issue, provided the availability of nontaxable forms is not discriminatory in favor of highly paid employees.

As the employee takes control over the decision of "what form" of compensation to take, the company's role changes significantly. Its major role will be controlling "how much" compensation. And that decision will be focused on total compensation.

4

Implementation Issues

Although the concept of flexibility in compensation and benefits has strong appeal, there are a number of issues that need to be addressed by employers planning to implement a program. One issue that looms large with many employers is how to communicate something as "complicated" as flexibility. Another is the possibility that some employees will make inappropriate selections from among the alternatives and that this will later cause dissatisfaction by the employee or embarrassment to the company. A further issue involves the possibility that employees will make selections which are "too smart" and cause additional costs through adverse selection (for example, employees with poor teeth will be the only ones to elect to participate in the dental plan although the pricing may have anticipated a "cross-section" of employees). A final area requiring consideration is the creation and maintenance of the necessary administrative processes for operating a flexible program.

COMMUNICATION

Under a flexible system, employees need more information and a better understanding of their benefits than usual. Because the concept represents a departure from what employees have been accustomed to, many will feel insecure about their ability to make decisions. Moreover, the concept can sometimes meet with employee suspicion—at least at the outset. The flexible system may be viewed by some employees as management's attempt to take something away or to cut costs. The communication process needs both to build credibility with employees and to increase their understanding of the program.

One way to accomplish these objectives is to break the communication process into manageable parts. For example, the stages of flexible communication might involve:

- *Pretesting with employees.* This is the stage for listening and reacting to employee attitudes about the concept of flexibility, about options that would make a program attractive, and about ways to introduce a new system.

  In addition to laying the groundwork for flexibility, the research stage will yield information critical to the design of a program. High-priority benefits can be identified. Different employee group reactions can be isolated. Some measure of later employee acceptance of the program can be gauged.
- *Announcing a flexible decision.* This is the stage for reporting results of the research phase to the workforce, for addressing employee concerns, for building in evidence of management support, and for cultivating the support of line and human resource managers.
- *Explaining the program.* This is the stage for educating all participants about the program and building enthusiasm, since employees will be asked to spend a considerable amount of time working through their individual decisions. Enough information needs to be provided for employees to make intelligent choices, but not so much as to confuse. Employees need to gain confidence in their decision-making abilities.
- *Enrolling employees.* This stage is a continuation of the education process, but focuses on the specifics of enrollment. Certain groups or locations may require special attention.
- *Following up.* Once the press of the first enrollment is over, the overall effort requires evaluation. This is the stage for fine-tuning or simplifying enrollment procedures, for redesigning forms to ease claims processing, and for providing required communica-

tion materials (summary plan descriptions, summary annual reports, and so on).

Clear and repeated communication is important if an organization is to help employees understand the concept of flexibility and how each of the options works.

POOR SELECTION

The possibility that employees will make poor choices exists in most benefit programs, but is accentuated in a flexible system. For example, most savings plans allow the employee to select from a number of investment options including company stock, a diversified equity account, a balanced stock/bond account, and a money market fund. At the end of most accounting periods, it is obvious, in retrospect, that most employees did not choose the options with the highest rate of return. Employees also make choices as to the level of optional contributory group life insurance or whether or not to participate in a contributory long-term disability plan.

The choices available under a flexible program are typically much broader, however, raising greater concerns that employees may make inappropriate decisions. Under a program with *complete* flexibility, for example, an employee might elect to take cash in lieu of any death benefits. The implications of these choices might be unacceptable.

The first line of defense to protect against problems in this area is to create a nonflexible core of basic benefits providing minimum levels of coverage in the benefit areas with greatest financial risk. The core might have catastrophic medical coverage, $10,000 of group life insurance, and the like. The core concept reduces the organization's concern with the consequences of employee choice.

A number of other tactics also help employees make intelligent choices:

- *Pretesting.* One purpose of pretesting is to identify what options appeal to employees and which ones are easily understood by them. Thus, the flexible program can be developed in a way that will minimize the potential of poor choices.

- *Enrollment Simulation.* An entire group may go through a simulation of the program prior to the real election. This helps employees understand how the process operates and provides training in handling the first real election. In addition, the simulation may provide data that will be helpful in the development of prices for options. It can also be used to test whether or not the actual enrollment is likely to meet any applicable IRS rules for nondiscrimination.
- *Error Detection.* Employees' choices can be reviewed (generally by computer) for logical sense. Did someone sign up for payroll deductions in excess of 10 percent of pay? Did a single employee choose family medical benefits? Error messages can be sent back to employees to check whether their selections really reflect their intent.

Analysis of elections made by employees in various organizations indicates that employees are able to take responsibility for their own benefits and exercise good judgment. Where communication has been well planned and implemented and where the benefit program has been simplified to the point where understanding can be created with reasonable effort, employees tend not to have significant problems making decisions about benefits. To some extent, this comes as no surprise; most employees have long been accustomed to making decisions on how to allocate their paychecks in a satisfactory manner.

ADVERSE SELECTION

The risk of adverse selection arises with insurance options, such as life insurance, health care benefits, and disability protection. If a choice is made available to employees for a fixed price, will those with a greater chance of incurring the risk select the option while those with a lesser chance spend their money elsewhere? If this occurs to a significant degree, the company could raise the price of the option to cover these additional costs. But this would tend to create even greater adverse selection in subsequent years as more of the "good risks" decide to avoid the higher cost option. Alternatively, the company may be forced to subsidize the option in order to encourage broad participation.

There is no single solution to the problems of adverse selection. However, a number of tactics can minimize its financial impact on the operation of a flexible program.

Grouping of Coverages

Some coverages cannot be written as separate options without involving adverse selection. For example, it is clearly not feasible to isolate maternity benefits as a separate benefit option since employees can easily classify themselves as potential users of the coverage. Therefore, only those likely to use the benefit would choose the option rather than a broad cross-section of employees. Vision care benefits are another example of this principle. Possible mechanisms to reduce (or eliminate) the impact of adverse selections in these coverages are (1) to include them in the set of core benefits or (2) to cluster several coverages together as a single option that will appeal to a broader group of employees.

Charging Less Than the True Cost

Some options will appeal to a broader group (and therefore be less likely to generate adverse selection costs) if they are priced at levels which are lower than their actual costs. Dental care may be a good example. Pricing a dental option at two-thirds of the expected cost will create a more attractive option and encourage greater participation, minimizing the potential adverse selection costs. Of course, simply lowering the option price would result in a significant employer subsidy for each employee who elects dental coverage. It is possible, however, to eliminate this subsidy or extra cost if dental benefits are included in the pre-flexible program but not in the core benefits. This can be done by generating flexible credits to give to employees to make up for the elimination of dental coverage which are equal to only two-thirds of the anticipated cost savings created.

Actual Cost Pricing

The plan can charge prices directly related to the amount of an individual's risk. For example, life insurance options can have prices based on age rather than a flat charge for all ages. This encourages younger employees to purchase coverage. The result should be broader participation that would reduce adverse selection. In addition, the plan can provide that an individual can opt for large amounts of additional life insurance only upon providing evidence of insurability or during specified open-enrollment periods.

Restrictions on Ability to Switch Options

Most flexible programs are designed to allow the employee to change options annually. Although this may be appropriate in most areas, it may lead to adverse selection within benefit areas where expenses are somewhat predictable and somewhat delayable. For example, an individual who is participating in the dental option this year may decide to visit the dentist in December to have any necessary work performed, opt out the dental plan next year, and attempt to put off his next visit to the dentist until January of the following year—after he re-enrolls in the dental option. Through this approach, the employee could have all dental expenses (except those which are of an emergency nature in the nonparticipating years) paid by the plan, even though he is only charged for the coverage every other year.

An effective way to minimize this risk would be to require that an employee who drops dental coverage would have to wait a minimum of two years before re-enrolling.

Moreover, some coverages are better provided on an individual basis than on a group basis. For example, if it is desirable to provide an option to increase retirement benefits, it may be more practical to provide the opportunity through an individual account savings plan rather than through purchasing additional pension units.

ADMINISTRATION

Another set of issues involves the additional effort and cost associated with administering a flexible program. Unquestionably, administrative tasks are both more numerous and more complicated. But the issue of complex administration is rapidly fading from an actual to a perceived problem.

One solution is to approach administration from a systems orientation. That is, reduce the task to a series of manageable, identifiable steps. In total, flexible administration involves three major functions:

1. Collecting data on each employee.
2. Assigning flexible credits to each employee, and tracking the options selected by each individual.
3. Paying individual claims.

In practice, two-thirds of the functions already are being performed through the normal operation of a conventional benefit program. For example, data on each employee (the input) typically is already available. For pension purposes, certain employee data is collected annually—social security number, date of birth, date of hire, sex, pay, and so on. Under a capital accumulation plan, individual account balances must be reported at least annually.

For welfare benefits (medical and life insurance, for example) the employer usually already tracks coverages, pay level, and so on. In effect, most of the input is available—often in a form that can be fed into a flexible compensation system.

Similarly, data is often already in a usable form on the output end. Either manual or computerized systems exist within a company to calculate and pay death, disability, medical, and dental claims. Some process also exists for tracking vacation time.

The missing element for a flexible system is the middle task—linking the input and the output through a system that computes and tracks individual choices. Several steps are involved: (1) determining individual credits, (2) recording individual elections, and (3) storing choices for eventual claims payment.

The critical element of the middle stage is the election process. Not only must enrollment tasks be performed, but extra care taken to assure that employees fully understand their alternatives. But a simple, logical series of checks and balances can help the election stage flow smoothly—and at the same time minimize the risk of poor employee choices. Consider the steps:

- The election form is sent to employees.
- The individual selects the options he or she wants, completes the form, and returns it for processing.

- The form is reviewed for accuracy and completeness. Logic tests are also used to verify the good sense of the decisions made.
- If no error is found, a report form is prepared and sent to the employee.
- The employee checks the report to verify that his decisions have been recorded correctly. If so, he signs the form and returns it, keeping one copy. He is now enrolled.

There are also ways to help those who fail to follow the process perfectly. If an error is found in the original form (such as selecting two medical options or choosing dependent death benefits for a single employee) the form is simply returned to the employee with a note explaining what is wrong, and requesting a new form.

If the employee changes his or her mind after seeing the report form, he or she can still make different selections and generate a new report form. Thus, the process has built-in safeguards and error checks to increase accuracy.

A number of employers are pursuing more streamlined approaches to bringing flexible systems on line. Instead of tackling flexibility in terms of many choices across all employee benefit areas, current practice tends toward starting with more limited selections within a few benefit areas. A more modest approach provides the company a chance to ease into the system, and at the same time gradually introduce employees to the decision-making process.

It should be noted that dealing with administration can loom as so large a spectre as to discourage even the most tentative venture into flexibility. Or administration can be made manageable and do-able. In the over 30 flexible systems currently on line, none was in so advanced a stage that administration posed no problem. Yet, once implementation had begun, each program went on to successful enrollment and operation.

5

Generations of Programs

Describing flexible programs is somewhat akin to describing the history of microprocessors. Developments occur so fast that one generation rapidly flows into another, with each past generation continuing in use. So far, four generations or approaches are discernible.

GENERATION ONE: SATISFACTION THROUGH INVOLVEMENT

As early as the 1950s, behavioral scientists were developing data showing that many employers were not getting maximum mileage for their expenditures on noncash compensation. Abraham Maslow developed the hierarchy of human needs, suggesting that an individual will concentrate on one rung of the ladder until satisfied before proceeding to the next. Until the employee has enough money in wages and enough security in benefits, he or she is unlikely to be interested in working toward the higher levels of satisfying ego needs and achieving self-actualization.

In the 1960s, compensation theories were developed that divided employee-relations activities into "motivators" and "dissatisfiers." Employee benefits were clearly in the second category. This implied that the absence of a decent set of benefits could hurt a company, but its presence would do little good.

It was against this background that the first experiments with flexibility took place. Cummins Engine established study groups and found positive interest in the idea of choice-making.

Although considerable work was done in developing a possible structure for a flexible program, other corporate realities interfered with the project. Management at Cummins Engine was forced to postpone the project in spite of favorable employee response.

In the 1960s, a large high-technology corporation set up random sample employee study groups to test the receptivity for choice-making. While there was some support for the concept, the timing was poor. Employees were accustomed to banner years, with 15 percent of pay contributed annually to their profit sharing plan and a host of other benefits. Choice-making seemed to be a negative concept when the employer already provided a full range of protection.

The first flexible programs came into being in the early 1970s. After considerable employee research, TRW's Defense and Space Systems Group determined that choice-making would be positively received and that the very act of involvement would stir positive employee reaction.

The company developed a series of choices within life insurance and medical benefits permitting an individual to opt up or down from the previous levels of coverage. If in the aggregate the employee chose coverages of less value than in effect previously, the difference would be paid in cash. If the employee chose benefits of greater worth than previously in effect, payroll deductions were required. TRW did not increase its cost for noncash compensation. Employee response was positive because individuals made decisions for themselves and perceived these decisions to be of greater value than the way the money had been spent previously.

Another flexible program was introduced at the same time at Educational Testing Service. This project started with a measurement of benefit costs at Educational Testing Service and other institutions. When the study revealed that Educational Testing Service was paying considerably less in payroll for benefits, they decided to catch up. However, instead of Educational Testing Service deciding where the extra money was to be spent, each participant was given a choice as to where the increase was to be allocated among a series of optional choices built on top of existing benefit levels. Random sample study groups were given an opportunity to contribute to the design of the program. As at TRW, the results showed a strong positive employee response. Since the organization was adding funds to the program, it was not surprising that employees found greater value. What was less predictable was the continuing positive response over time when Educational Testing Service stopped making further additions. This is an example of positive employee response not always being correlated with the amount of money being spent. What can be concluded about the characteristics of Generation One flexible programs?

- The first two programs had unusual "social" situations. TRW was long known as a human resource innovator. The nature of Educational Testing Service was small, and academic—exactly the type of environment where independent choice-making could be expected to fit.
- Flexible development was stimulated by a desire to involve employees in the belief that this would produce more positive attitudes toward the organization.
- Employees participated not only in the exercise of individual choice but in the design of the options themselves. This successful participation set a precedent that has been followed in virtually every flexible program developed to date.
- The programs were arranged so there was no possible take-away for employees. Either the individual could return to the program previously in effect at no additional personal cost, or the employee was actually given more value.

GENERATION TWO: APPLICATION TO BROADER INDUSTRY

Despite the initial successes of the first two flexible programs, application did not spread rapidly. One reason for this was technical—the ERISA ban on development of new plans permitting employee choice-making. A more important reason was that companies were not motivated strongly enough to justify the apparent complexities in the flexible approach. The advantages of employee involvement appeared secondary in importance to providing steady work and increasing incomes in a period of economic uncertainty. A related reason was the prevailing attitude among benefit managers and technicians that flexibility was for the "unusual" situation—the unique workforce or the company with a small existing level of benefits. Since most organizations were not in that situation, flexibility was considered inappropriate.

One organization turned these attitudes around virtually by itself. In 1978, American Can Company established a flexible program with a wide variety of choices in virtually all benefit areas. It avoided the problem of the ban under Section 2006 of ERISA by providing that no choice could involve cash or taxable benefits. Elaboration of the American Can experience is well deserved because this program represented a breakthrough in many ways. American Can's program demonstrated that:

- A flexible program could be operated within the ban under Section 2006 of ERISA.
- An existing benefit program with high costs could be split into nonflexible and flexible portions, rather than merely adding flexibility on top of an existing set of benefits.
- The concept of "take-away" was acceptable to employees so long as they had an opportunity to buy back their old coverage with the amount of flexible credits provided them.
- First-dollar medical benefits were not necessarily considered sacred in the eyes of employees. Only about 10 percent spent enough credits to buy back their previous first-dollar medical coverage, while the remaining 90 percent found deductibles acceptable if the value saved could be spent in another form.
- A large organization could establish and administer a flexible program with a wide variety of choices. Administration lent itself easily to computerization, sharply limiting increased costs.
- The company added another objective to the familiar one of maximizing employee satisfaction. American Can viewed flexibility as having the potential to help control future increases in benefit costs. By separating the formula for determining flexible credits from the pricing structure of options, some of the built-in escalation in benefit costs could be curbed.

American Can's contribution to the history of flexibility lay in demonstrating that this approach held significant potential for large organizations with well-developed benefit programs. Flexibility was no longer restricted to the unique organization motivated only to maximize employee satisfaction. American Can made flexibility attractive to the hard-nosed business person and the streetwise but skeptical production foreman.

GENERATION THREE: DIVERSIFICATION AND ENLARGEMENT

As knowledge spread of what American Can had done, some organizations studied whether that precise program could be installed. Herein lies an irony. Flexibility was born as a method of "turning people on" by giving them a chance to elect what they want, not to follow a pattern laid down by other employers.

The 1978 Revenue Act spurred development of what might be called a new approach to flexible programs. The underlying attitude is that flexibility is a *system* rather than a *program*. It is a method of paying compensation and benefits that consists of part fixed and part flexible items. The system may be applied in many ways: to groups of differing size, to programs of differing costs, and to benefit areas of differing breadth. It is a way of paying people, and *diversity* is its basic characteristic.

The way in which it is applied in any one organization depends upon the organization's broad human resource goals as well as its benefit objectives.

There are now many organizations in addition to TRW, Educational Testing Service, and American Can that have implemented flexible programs or announced an implementation date to employees. Within this group there are significant differences in employee population, type of business, structure of program, and reasons for introduction. One way to categorize this diversity is by program structure. Moving from the simplest to the most complex, there are about five recognizable plan categories.

1. Reimbursement Accounts

In the prototype reimbursement account program, installed at Hewitt Associates in 1980, employees are given an annual flexible credit reserve based on length of service. The reserve can be allocated to pay certain medical, dental, and legal expenses not covered by the group program. These expenses are limited to those which are deductible business expenses of the organization and are not taxable income to the employee. Unused credits flow into a capital accumulation plan at year-end.

This model, with some variations, has been implemented by Highland Park Hospital in Chicago for its 1,000 part-time and full-time employees and by Simpson Industries, a Michigan auto-parts maker, for about 400 employees.

This approach lends itself to organizations that wish to make some benefits available in such ancillary areas as dental, vision, hearing, and legal, but feel that employees should have the opportunity to choose the items they can use. It also can be one element of a more complete flexible program that offers choices among basic benefit areas as well.

2. Health Care Versus Cash or Deferred Compensation

PepsiCo's flexible program, started in June of 1980, was unique in covering only a limited area: health care. Choices consisted of three medical plans, two dental plans, a vision and hearing plan, and cash. Today there are 10,000 nonunion employees from PepsiCo Corporation, Pepsi-Cola, North American Van Lines, and Taco Bell participating in the program. Employee acceptance has been good even though the amount of additional company contribution is limited.

In September 1981, Little Company of Mary Hospital in the Los Angeles area offered 1,300 full-time and part-time employees an opportunity to choose between a standard benefit package that included medical, dental, vision, and life insurance coverage and a standard package including catastrophic medical coverage, but no dental, vision, or life insurance. Those who choose the second alternative receive a cash payment of $500 per year. The hospital designed this program in recognition that a large portion of its employee group were second wage earners covered for medical benefits under a spouse's plan.

In January of 1982, Arcata Corporation introduced a trade-off between medical and dental coverage and vacation at its book division in Kingsport, Tennessee. A total of 3,200 salaried and hourly workers at this nonunionized operation will test the concept before company-wide application is decided upon. Each of these organizations chose to make its medical benefits more flexible, probably in recognition that employees' needs for protection vary most dramatically in this area. Of course each also has the potential to expand their program with other benefit choices if it seems appropriate.

3. Welfare Benefits Only

In October 1981, Johnson Controls, Inc., a maker of environmental control systems, offered 8,200 salaried employees a program of choices among certain welfare benefits. Employees select from among a series of medical, dental, life, travel accident, and accidental death and dismemberment benefits.

This program grew out of an initial plan to move toward flexible benefits, followed by an acquisition that made it necessary to offer a new common program to two employee groups with different existing benefit packages. If results of this effort continue to be successful, attention will be directed to expanding the program into additional benefit areas and deferred compensation.

4. Welfare Benefits Versus Cash, Plus Welfare Benefits Versus Deferred Compensation

Another unique program, introduced by a Minnesota utility, was designed to offer trade-offs between cash, welfare benefits, and retirement benefits before the 1978 Revenue Act was amended to permit three-way trade-offs in a single plan. Consequently, their program has two modules. One allows choices between death benefits and cash; the other allows trade-offs between retirement benefits and cash.

Since the passage of the Miscellaneous Revenue Act of 1980, it was no longer necessary to separate these choices into modules.

5. Welfare Benefits Versus Deferred Compensation

This type of plan, for which American Can is the prototype, has spread to at least three other organizations.

In January 1981, Northern States Power Company in Minneapolis started a program for 3,300 nonunion employees that offers choices among welfare benefits and deferred compensation (with no cash choice). However, some features were unique at that time to Northern States Power.

- Trade-offs between hard dollar benefits and soft dollar time off are incorporated, with some of the flexible credits derived from a reduction in vacation time. The employee can either "buy back" the vacation time or use those credits to buy hard dollar benefits.
- Purchasing additional pension units is incorporated in the program. The pension benefit was reduced and the employee has an opportunity to buy it back.

Later in 1981, Morgan Stanley & Co. followed a similar format but instead of automatically shrinking basic benefits to create its flexible credit pool, management left it to each employee to shrink an existing benefit if he or she wanted more of another.

Loews Corporation has also enrolled employees in a program that became effective in January 1982. The program, which covers 3,500 salaried employees, offers choices of welfare benefits, vacation, and deferred compensation. Its purpose is to appeal to the diverse needs of the workforce and maximize the perceived value of the benefit program.

The contribution being made by these new programs is to demonstrate that flexibility can be structured in a wide variety of ways and applied in widely different circumstances.

GENERATION FOUR: EXPANSION OF OBJECTIVES

We are seeing the emergence of a new approach in flexible benefit systems. The distinguishing characteristic is the use of flexibility to accomplish very specific purposes, above and beyond splitting a benefit program into fixed and flexible portions and achieving ends related to benefits. These new systems may be constructed along the lines of earlier models, but they have features that distinguish them as having additional goals.

For example, flexible systems are now being viewed by two organizations as an opportunity to create greater equality in compensation between single and married employees. In one case, Girard Bank of Philadelphia, the nonflexible medical core provides hospital benefits for employees only. Flexible options include major medical and dental benefits for employees and major medical and dental benefits for dependents. In another case, a major midwestern manufacturer, the amount of flexible credits is the same whether the person is single or married. This means that the married person must spend more money to cover dependents because the price of covering a family is greater than the price for covering an individual. Equality of compensation is a goal at these organizations because they believe that differences in compensation levels based on marital status are no longer acceptable. The flexible system provides a good mechanism to accomplish this purpose.

Another example of Generation Four is a program still in the developmental stage. In this company, the goal is to underline the concept of total compensation by expressing future compensation increases in total form and permitting the individual to divide them among savings, flexible credits, additional time off, and increases in cash compensation. This company believes that if the employee sees total compensation increase, the company will receive more credit for the amount being spent. The organization also wants to emphasize individuality and initiative as important values. Here again, the goals extend beyond the boundaries of benefits, and flexibility is serving as the system for helping the organization achieve them.

Another group of programs currently coming on line places greater emphasis on increasing the tax-effectiveness of compensation. Again, Girard Bank of Philadelphia is an example. The Girard program offers choices among welfare benefits, vacation, and deferred compensation. One of the original objectives was to permit a more tax-effective reallocation of compensation. By converting a portion of a large profit sharing plan into flexible credits that can be used to fund welfare contributions, employees do not have to use aftertax payroll dollars for that purpose.

Another example of this generation of flexible programs is the much-discussed 401(k) plan. Since choice about form of pay is offered, a cash or deferred plan fits neatly into the concept of flexible compensation. The employee is picking the form of compensation. But the employer's cost is not increased automatically as a result of choice being made available.

Effective January 1, 1982, Honeywell has implemented a Section 401(k) cash or deferred profit sharing arrangement. Under this plan, employees may elect to reduce their pay up to 4 percent with the amount of reduction being funneled into a profit sharing trust. At mid-year 1982, over 50 percent of Honeywell's 60,000 salaried employees had elected to participate in the salary reduction program.

A major supplier to the petroleum industry is coming on line with a program intended simply to convert aftertax employee contributions to a benefit program into beforetax contributions under Section 125 of the Code. A number of employers are using both Sections 125 and 401(k) to achieve tax-effectiveness. Some of these organizations may not yet have fully embraced the concept of flexible compensation, but they are moving toward it at their own pace.

GENERATION FIVE: THE SHAPE OF THINGS TO COME?

Over the past decade, tremendous change has taken place in the way flexible systems are structured. A chancy but instructive exercise might be to predict the shape of flexible systems yet to come.

An idea meriting some consideration is the concept of "flexible pay" within total compensation. Already the line of distinction between "pay" and "benefits" is beginning to blur. For a number of years, organizations have presented employees with benefit statements in an effort to acquaint them with the full value of their total compensation. Future flexible systems may represent a further step toward integration of all amounts spent for pay and security needs.

Flexible pay would represent a key element of total compensation.

Exhibit 2. Total compensation.

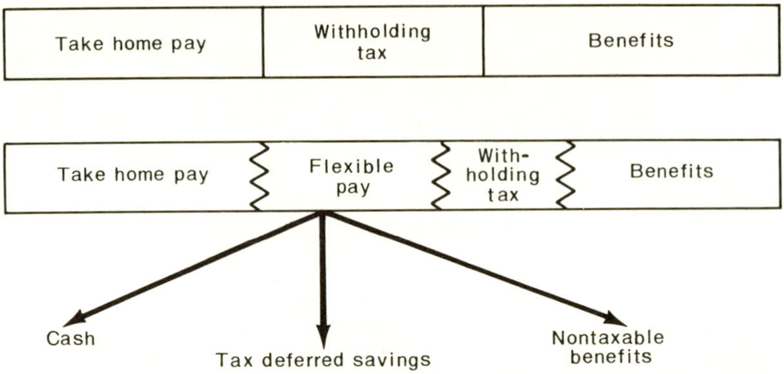

An employee would know how much of total compensation is paid as annual salary and how much would be required to provide basic benefit protection. But between the two extremes would be an amount of pay that could be used to provide additional benefit protection, channeled into tax-deferred savings, or taken in cash. Depending on how the employee elected to spend the flexible pay, the amount of income tax liability would vary. As Exhibit 2 illustrates, the line of demarcation between pay and benefits has virtually been eliminated, forcing recognition of total compensation.

Many more organizations are exploring the addition of flexibility to their benefit programs. Some have studied the idea and rejected it temporarily. Their reasons include technical inability to administer the program, discomfort that regulations have not been finalized, and concern about the ability to control adverse selection or poor employee choices. In some cases, employees have expressed distrust of the company's intentions or unwillingness to choose among benefits which they believe the company should fund for everyone. Finally, there are organizations where management believes its current benefit strategy is so effective that no improvements can be made.

6

Summing Up

One point about the development of flexible compensation to date requires reiteration. Flexibility is being viewed as a system to accomplish various organizational goals and objectives. It is *not* a type of benefit program that carries with it a complicated set of options and produces an administrative nightmare. Instead, flexible compensation is a different way to deliver compensation and benefits. The approach permits an employer to separate decisions on form of compensation and levels of cost.

Flexible systems are being shaped and influenced by important realities:

- *Favorable Employee Attitudes.* Employees like choice. They appreciate the opportunity to meet their own needs. When given the chance to buy back or restore a preflexible program, relatively few elect to do so.

  Moreover, attitudes seem to remain favorable for long periods. Even after programs are in operation for some years, employees believe their program is better than those covering their counterparts elsewhere, even though employer expenditures may escalate more slowly. As long as options are in areas deemed important to employees, employer cost takes a backseat to the opportunity to meet individual needs.

- *Cost Containment.* In a conventional program, employer alternatives for cost control include placing a freeze on new benefits, taking away or cutting back existing coverages, or asking for larger employee contributions. None of these is particularly palatable to the employee, and companies have been reluctant to push too hard in these directions. A flexible program permits the employer to strive for cost control in a way that is less painful for employees. Choice-making enables an employer to meet the needs and preferences of a diverse workforce without so extensive a cost commitment.
- *Tax-Effectiveness.* Employees at all earnings levels are tax conscious so tax-effective benefits and savings are well received. As Congress continues to expand the list of items eligible for tax-favored status, pressure on the employer for "more" is likely to rise. Considering that further expansion of total compensation costs is unlikely in the current environment, having employees elect among taxable and nontaxable options seems a plausible response.

Organizations have different goals and motivations for exploring flexibility. Some will retain conventional structures under which the organization assumes responsibility for allocation of total compensation amounts. Others will move to systems under which employees can make choices. For these employers, flexibility appears to be a good way to involve employees in pay and benefit decisions, to help the organization receive value for its total compensation expenditures, and to place some limits on the organization's future increases in benefit costs.